1

A Piece Of Me

Honey I Bought This For You

ACNOWLEDGEMENT
I Would Like To Thank My Lord
And Savior Jesus Christ
FOR ALL THAT HE HAS
Given Me.
Thanking God I Am
For My Talents and Gifts.
I Recognize That The Lord Gave
Me This Gift, Which Allows Me To
Share With Children And
Everyone That Participates In The
Reading Of The Literary Material
That I Produce Through The
Commission Of God.

Thank You Lord God

I Will Forever Be Grateful
For Your Trust In Me
Pamela Denise Brown

Books Speak For You books may be ordered through
booksellers or by contacting:
Books Speak For You Educational Publishing
Booksspeakforyou.com, Pamelainthelight.com
267-318-8933
The views expressed in this work are solely those of
the author.
Any illustration provided by iStock and such images
are being used for illustrative purposes.
Certain stock imagery © iStock.
ISBN: 978-1-64050-001-3

Printed in the United States Of America

God Woke Me Up

And I'm sharing this with you...

I feel the greatness of God and his Love for me pushing me to a place where He can be Glorified...

Grasping for understanding in my mind...
a divine download has occurred and as it is archived in my mind for a purpose..
I serve until the delivery of this word can be revealed...
I was called out of my sleep just to worship...
I acknowledge the gifted word, because I am a servant chose to serve..
 a trusted source to give God Glory in what Goad has supernaturally given me to do..

When the act of this Devine download allows my flesh to partake we will see God Glorified in it...

For only God can get the credit for such a supernatural move that causes a man to gain wealth unbeknown to him..

I accept my calling to be a distributor of God's goodness and wait for the manifestation of what has spiritually been done..

All honor all glory goes to God...

As God continues to minister to my being, I lay here in receipt of the deposit...

Should I cry.. for even the writing of this is a command that moved me.. God wants to prove himself mighty in the lives of His people. We can no longer hold up the line with our disobedience, lest we block the recipients who are to benefit from what God told His chosen to do. Amen God the Sprit rest in me.
January 11, 2017 3:48 a.m.

POETRY

Honey

I

Bought

This For

You

Honey I bought this for you...

I was thinking about YOU, I saw you in my head...

The vision of you made me think of you, your smile,

your ability to listen to everything I say without interrupting me,

your ability to laugh when you feel like crying,

the strength you display every morning when you get up and take care of me and the children.....

I bought this for you...

I was thinking about you,

I saw you glance back at me as you walked out the door,

you assured me that I was still the apple of your eye,

we were one...

I felt secure and safe,

I was honored...
That look said,
I can't wait to see you again,
fall in your arms,
lay on your chess,
play in my hair...

Honey I bought this for you...

I thought about you while I was in the shower,
I tried to come up with things to make you feel better to let you know I cared,

I wanted to let you know that I still get butterflies when I think about you,
I long everyday to see you,
after work talk to you,
takes long walks with you
or
just simply lay beside you...

I bought this for you...

I imagined you with your eyes closed in
the bathtub,
bathing,
relaxing,
preparing to see me...
to hold me,
to be with me,
to care for me and to love me...

I bought this for you...

I knew you would enjoy this...
I don't know how you really think ,
but I know I love you,
I'll do anything for you, because I enjoy
you,
I'm still in love with you...

Honey I bought this for you...

I watched you walk down the driveway...
I saw you get in your car...
and then I watched you drive away...

After you left I took a whiff of your perfume,
I wanted to capture you in the scent you wore...

I looked in the closet and found the dress
I love seeing you in ...
it was modest and mature...

I bought this for you, because I wanted you to know I'm thinking about you,
I'll always be here psychologically for you,
emotionally and spiritually too...

Honey I bought this book for you.

What SUCCESS Means To Me

SUCCESS For Me Is Obedience to
God
Fulfillment of the work God has
chosen for me to do.

SUCCESS For Me is being able to
have Self-control...
To show genuine Love constantly
towards others
To embrace people I don't know
without judging them.

SUCCESS for me is to wake up
every morning with the ability to
lift my head..
and my heart
In Praise to God
for my NEW Awakening.

SUCCESS for me, Pamela I AM,
is to begin my day focusing on
how to please God
And
how to make life better for
someone else with my presence.
SUCCESS for me is not hurting
people with MY
Words
And
MY Actions.

SUCCESS for me is to always
exhibit Christ.

SUCCESS for me is to gain a
full understanding of
WHO I AM
and
WHAT GOD
has chosen for me.

SUCCESS for me is to
KNOW
WHO I AM
In Christ
and
become who
God
wants me to be.

SUCCESS for me is to lay myself
down in all aspects
And
to always deny myself
for the benefit
of
others.

SUCCESS for me is to
CAPTURE
Myself
In the Vision of God's EYE
And
Finally Become Me.
That's what I CALL SUCCESS!!!!!!!

I Want To Whisper In Your Ear

I Want To Whisper

In

Your ear

Tell you that I love you

let you know that you make

me feel safe

inform you

that I'm appreciative of

you

Express to

you

the depth of my love

share my dreams with you.

I Want To Whisper

In

Your Ear

Sentiments of

Love

sing softly to

you

Speak continued life in you

Whisper in

your ear

I'm here for

you

Tell you again

and again

how much I

love you

That I want to spend my life

with

you

I Want To Whisper In Your
Ear

Let you know

I'm glad I waited for you

Advise

you

that I'll always

exhibit patience

with you

understanding

is

what I'll give to

you

I will always

listen to

you

and

never stop

being a friend to you.

I Want To Whisper In Your

Ear

That I thank

God

over and over for

you

I'll submit

to you

Walk beside

You

uphold

you

and lift you up

Because I love that

God

picked me for you.

I Want To Whisper In Your
Ear.

POWER

POWER

We Feel Without Touch...

We See Without Sight...

A Force From A POWER

We Do Not Control...

We Love Without Reason...

We Cooperate Without
Comprehension...

A Force Of Power We Do Not
Control...

A Decree Before Our
Creation...

A Command Before Our
Time

That Found Us

In Time

And

Brought Us Together...

We Move Standing Still...

We Communicate Without
Words...

A Force From A POWER

We Do Not Control...

WOMAN

Woman

God Made Me

Created Me According To

Genesis

2 Not 3

Listen Ladies

I'll Explain Your Position
To You

I'll Start In Genesis 2 and
22

²² And the rib that

the LORD God had taken

from the man he made

into a woman and

brought her to the

man. [23] Then the man

said,

"This at last is bone of

my bones

and flesh of my flesh;

she shall be called

Woman,

because she was taken

out of Man."

WOMAN

I Want To Explain This

Further To You

God Called You

To Be A Queen

Not Some

Mean Woman That

Screams And Screams

And

Tares The Family Apart

Because You Don't Want
To Do Your Part

Yes You Are A Queen

Perhaps

An

Empress

A Teacher

A Helpmate

And A Doctor

Sometimes Too

Being A Woman Is A

Honor

Not A Chore

WE Motivate Encourage

And

Softly Roar

Never Out Of Control

Never Out Of Line

Always, Always
Considering Others
ALWAYS

Gently, Softy

Loving And Kind

WOMAN

Let Me Educate You

Enhance Your Mind

Set The Stage

Present To You

What I Know

Show You

The Meaning Of A

Woman

From My

Perspective View

Perhaps It Will Be A

Mirrored View Of You

Of Me

Let Me Enhance Your

Mind

Woman

Set The Stage

Present To You

Show You

The Meaning Of Life

In My Mirrored View

As I Present

And

Make Myself Available To

You

Woman

Let Me

Enhance Your Mind

Ameliorate You

Amend You

Enrich Your Life

To Help And

Refine You....

In Christ That Is

So You Can See

The Woman

That God Made

In You And In Me

Woman

Let Me

Enhance Your Mind

Upgrade, Revamp,

Rehabilitate

And

Revise You

To Boost You

Fortify, Polish, Hone

And

Give You

A Touch Up

To Improve

The Quality Of Life

For You

The Life That God

Has Given

You

Given Me

WOMAN

Why Can't

You See

You Don't Have To Holler

Scream

Or Shout

You're Heard

You're Seen

You're The

Woman

And

You Have Clout

You Have Strength

You Have Passion

You Have

Everything

God Gave

When He Created You

YOU WOMAN

ARE

Precious

And

You Should

Believe In You

Woman

As I Stand Here AND

Encourage

Enlighten

AND

Give To You

Words To

Inspire

Show Love

AND

Celebrate

YOU

I Also Warn

You

Of Things

That Perhaps

You Can't See

The Things

That Trap

Tangle

And

Destroy

YOU

This Is Just

Not

About

Uplifting

Encouraging

And

Motivating

You

This Is To

Also

Warn And Make You

Pay Attention

To

You

THE WOMAN

God Wants To

Come Forth

While

He Lives In You

WOMAN

What Is Change?

What Is Change?

Does it cause a man to

live different

act different

talk different

dress different

not be the same

What is change?

Does it cause a man to treat
people different love different

have different views

respond different

believe different

What is change?

I Woke

Up To

You

I Woke Up To You

Your Eyes

Your Mouth

Your Face

Your Smile

I Woke Up To You

Your Love

Your Embrace

Your Touch

The Warmth Of Your
Body

I Woke Up To You

Your Ideas

Your Imagination

Your Visions

Your Dreams

I Woke Up To You

Your Encouragement

Your Passion

Your Faith

Your Hope

I Woke Up To You

I Can Still Smell You

I can still smell you...

Your Scent Means You're
Here With Me...

Apple Wood...

The Ocean...

Winter...

Purity In The Rain...

I Can Still Smell You...

I like that...

Simple Words...

I'm Not Thinking Hard
Today...

I Can Still Smell You...

I'm Going Crazy...

Only Because

I Want To...

I'm Dancing

In The Mirror

Thinking About You...

I'm Wearing Your

Glasses...

I See You

Looking At Me...

The Mirror View

Of You

Seeing Me

With Your Glasses On Is

Sensational...

I Can Still Smell You...

I Inhale Your Scent Like
Fresh Air

And I'm Refreshed...

I Feel So Good...

I Stretch When I Think
About You...

I'm Prepared To

Continue To Love You...

Sit With You

I Can Still Smell You...

I'm Clinching...

Everything Is Ok....

It's The Simple Things

I Enjoy...

I Want To Keep It That

Way...

I Can Still Smell You...

Your Smile

Has

Captured

Me

Your Smile Has Captured Me

in the warmth of your embrace.

Your cheeks raised,

The gleam brightened

in your smile,

your eyes alert,

Enduring it is to see.

Your smile has captured me.

Your Smile Has Captured Me,

I turned around

and saw you looking.

I met your eyes first,

Slowly rising

those cheeks again,

excited you were to see me,

frozen in disbelief,

Reunited again.

The emotions you held within.

Your smile has captured me.

Your Smile Has Captured Me,

I was awakened by your laugher...

You stared at me as I slept.

You chuckled,

I rose......

The innocence in your eyes

made me smile,

you smiled back.

Your smile has captured me.

Your Smile Has Captured Me,

In the still of the day,

We shared a pitcher

of lemonade,

it cooled us both off...

We laid under the hot sun and

tried to stare at it together.

Laughing,

we were blinded

at the same time

in the stare

trying to recapture

each other

in sight,

We closed our eyes

and

opened them again,

hoping to see each other clearly.

Your smile has captured me.

Your Smile Has Captured Me,

We sang a song together,

reminiscing on the good times

we shared

Praising God.

I sang out loud

with a terrible voice,

JESUS I LOVE YOU,

You looked,

Paused in your stare,

The comfort I demonstrated

singing the song

out of tune

surprised you,

as I sang it to you without

fear…….

You joined in….

.happy to be a part of

what made me happy.

Your smile has captured me.

Your Smile Has Captured Me,

I see you in my mirror view,

you're following me to the mall

I decided to take the lead

and you let me.

Assured that I knew the way,

you're laughing

And

I'm dialing you as we drive,

I SEE YOU

You're ok with taking a back seat

and letting me lead.

We get out the car,

you ask am I ok,

You laugh,

I stare for a second,

raise my eyebrow and say,

"so you thought I didn't know

where I was going",

You brush my hair back

And

say to me softly,

I have confidence in you,

If you were lost,

you would have asked

for directions.

Smiling WE ARE at each other,

happy to share another day.

Your smile has captured me.

Your Smile Has Captured Me,

It's late and I'm in your arms.

My tired eyes close,

You carry me to bed

and

as you tuck me in,

I raise my eyes

to gain another

LOOK

smiling

Your smile has captured me

QUOTES

Answers come in the still of
your mind

In the still of the moment
rested within

February 16, 2017

Read Yourself

Into Success

February 16, 2017

Encouragement

Is Understanding

That Encouraging Words

Are Echoes Of Sentiments

You First Send

To Yourself

August 11, 2016 — 2:03 am

My Life Means Something

Because It Matters

To Me

August 11, 2016 — 1:55 am

"In The View Of What You
Do
The Abyss Captures You,
My Moral Depths"

"We are At Best
keepers of Ourselves
It is the Drive Of That
KNOWLEDGE
That should drive us to
succeed
In a Heightened View
we are
isolated individuals
that will be rewarded
for our own accomplishments
July 8, 2016- 4:12 pm

Life Isn't That Complicated

It's That Fact That We Must
Change Our Life

To Live A Complicated Free
One

July 10, 2016

With Even Strokes

Caress The Mind

With Gentle Words

Handle A Child

With Excitement

Finish The Race

With Commitment

Help A Child Keep The Pace

LOVE IS EVERLASTING
WITH GOD

July 3, 2016 @ 10:06 pm.

Wisdom Is When

You Get To The Point

That It's Better

To Slow Down

And

Make The Right Choices

Than To Claim

You're Smart And

Keep Making The Same

Mistakes

My Conversations Are Different

But My Message Is The Same

I Have A Drive

That's Driven

By The Completion Of Gods
Work

In Me

When You Can Think

Of A Way

To Enhance The Mind

Of People

That Would Otherwise

Be Deprived

It Is Then

That Your Own Mind

Is Being Enhanced

11/21/2015- 1:40 a.m.

If To Educate

Is Your Objective

Than To Learn

Should Be Your

AIM...

11/21/2015 – 1:41 am

Moving In

The Difficult Times

Are Movements

Of Success

For To Be Still

Is Defeat

To Persevere Is To Conquer

11/21/2015-1:46 am

I Am Myself

Always Trying To Know Who

I Am

11/21/2015 -1:53 am

If I Can't See

The Need

In Others

I Am A Blind Person

Only

Pretending

To Have Sight

11/21/2015-1:58 am

The Greatest Love Story

Ever Told,

Is To Love In Separation

And

Be Brought Back Together

Apart

11/21/2015 1:59 am

When You Think

You Have Really

Been Stretched

Think Again...

Once You Reach Your Limit

You Won't Have To Think

11/21/2015 2:06 a.m.

Failure Is Not

An Option

There Is No Failure

In Life

Life Itself Is Won

In Understanding

To Fail Is Not

A Part Of Life

To Think One Has Failed

Means To Believe

God Is Not God

11/21/2015

If You're In A

"CROWDED"

Room

And

A Child Is Sitting

"ALONE"

That Can Only Mean

The Room Is

EMPTY

11/21/2015 1:42a.m.

Children Stand Silently

Trying To Open

A Door

That Cannot Be Opened

With Hands

11/23/2015 11:18

am

Preparing Children Now

Is To Prepare Them

For The Future

Not Waiting

For The Future

To Prepare

11/21/2015 2:13 am

Wisdom Is Using Wisely

The Lessons

In Life

To Be Wise

11/21/2015 2:14 am

To Be Patient

Is To Exercise

A Practice

Without Complaint

For Patience Is Accepting The

Idea

That You Have To

Wait

11/21/2015 2:16 am

Love Is Learning

That The Expression Of Love

Deserves Freedom

To Love

11/21/201 2:17 am

If You Really Want To

Enhance The Life

Of A Child

Your First Step

Is To See Yourself

Like A Child

And Then

Approach The Child Like You

See

Yourself

11/21/2015 2:22 am.

Obedience

Is Understanding

That You

Don't Need

To

Understand

11/21/2015-2:23 am

The Important Things

In Life

Are Not

Written Down

On Paper

They're Written

In Your Heart

11/23/2015-11:20 am

Intelligence Can Be

Accomplished

Through

Continued Learning

Being Intelligent

Is Applied

Through Understanding

That Intelligence

Is Nothing

If You Don't Have

A Heart

11/23/2015-11:21 am

If It Is Wealth

You Seek

In Adding Up Numbers

In An Account

You Will Never

Be Rich

11/23/2015-11:23 am

If You Can Walk By

A Person In Need

And

Look Down At Them

You Can't See Yourself

Everybody Needs Someone

11/23/2015-11:23 am

To Help Someone Is To

Actually

Help Yourself

If You're In A Position

To Help

You already Know

That In Order To Maintain

That Position

You Have To See Yourself

In Need

11/23/215-11:25 am

Someone Told Me Once

Cooperation

Does Not Require

Comprehension

........ahhhhh was it you

Shawn

11/23/2015-10:41 p.m.

When You Look

In The Mirror

You Should See Yourself

Not A Stranger

11/23/2015–10:42 pm

Common Sense

Is Knowing

That Everything

Doesn't Always

Make Sense

11/23/2015–10:43 pm

If God Delivered You

Then Why

Do You

Walk Around Looking Like

A Prisoner?

11/23/2015–10:43 pm

If You're Free
Why Do You Talk Like Your
Bound?
11/23/2105-10:44 pm

Surrendering

Is Having

Control

11/23/2015 – 1045 pm

Hatred

The World's Biggest

Enemy

July 23, 2016

THE LETTER I RECEIVED FROM THE PRESIDENT

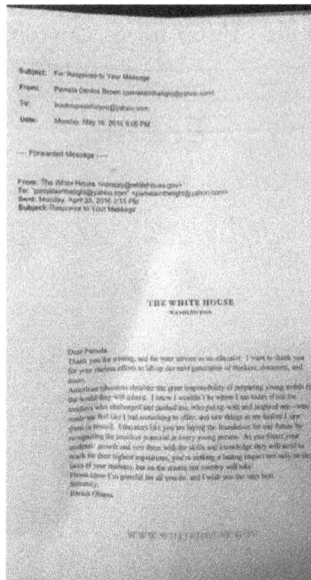

124

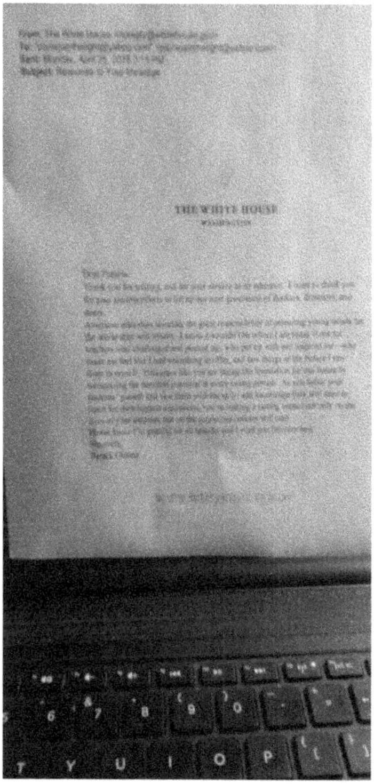

From: The White House <noreply@whitehouse.gov>
To: [email]
Sent: Monday, April 25, 2016 1:14 PM
Subject: Reponse to Your Message

THE WHITE HOUSE
WASHINGTON

Dear Patrick,

Thank you for writing, and for your desire to be educated. I want to thank you for your contribution to lift up our next generation of leaders, thinkers, and doers.

[remainder of letter illegible]

Sincerely,

Barack Obama

Thank You

Thank You

Thank You

Thank You

Thank You

Thank You

Thank You

I May Be Contacted

@ 267-318-8933

Bookspeakforyou@yahoo.com

(email)

Bookspeakforyou.com (website)

I Would Like To

Acknowledge Three Special People That Journeyed
Together Apart
Apart Together
Through The Process Of My Commission
Thank You
Queen Ella Brown
Sheranda Myers
AND
Shawn Richard Johnson

To My Mother

As a child, I woke up, I smiled and I was always eager to BE, to EXIST, to ADVENTURE, to DREAM, to DISCOVER, to PROPEL and to LEAD. Never was I ever willing to LISTEN... but one day I did and it changed my life. I grew up and life was introduced by the life I lead to me.

My life after your hand in it took many turns, a lot of good, a little bad and some ugly... but what makes it so Remarkable is that I Enjoyed It All.

127

There was something about the trials I went through that always allowed me to reach within myself and pull out a new me. I was often intrigued by my ability to keep rising after a fall.

As a family, we ate breakfast, lunch & dinner together... in the morning I would rise to shined shoes from my father outside my door, you contributed to that. As we ate dinner together, I watched the joy and excitement you had on your face as you prepared our meals. And it gave me joy. You lovingly baked sheet cakes and on all of our birthdays, there was a tradition that happy birthday be written in M & M's... you knew I didn't like them, but every year you did it anyway. I finally stopped complaining, because I knew it was done by a love I could not control.

As a mother, you made me and my sisters dresses every day with bows on them and every Christmas our gift boxes were evenly lined up to the ceiling.

You took pride in everything you did. We took summer vacations as a family every summer and on income tax day every year we had a new car... I remember that...

you were so caring and always filled our house with all of our cousins... I hated that, every weekend they were over, acting like you were there mother, cousin Shawn, Nana, Tracey, Dawn, John, Joe, Marty, Manny, Boo, Jaletti, Stacy, Shukria and my dad's favorite, Butter. This was family, your family. I didn't understand it early on, but then I realized you wanted to give to others, what you gave to us... so the love was shared and finally I began to appreciate who you were. I have never seen anyone give the way you have of herself... you've only had one man in your life and when he passed 22 years ago, you remained committed to God.

I have watched you serve in churches from a usher to the bathroom cleaner, to a evangelist, to a missionary, to a minster than promoted to Pastor.

You put my sister and I in ballet school and during our recital I couldn't remember what to do. It didn't matter, your love was orchestrated so well by everything you did, even our friends thought we were royalty. As a mother, you always told us to never settle, because in our home failure was not an option. We all succeeded through school and you can stick your chest out for that.

You travelled the world in ministry to help others and even was in Korea when they tore down the wall.

Then, I grew up and your conversations changed I got to the point that I didn't want to hear anything else you had to say, but then you said something that I could not ignore, my spirit couldn't ignore it, my creation couldn't ignore it, my intelligence couldn't ignore it and I had to listen.

You told me that I didn't have to listen to you, you told me that God told you to stop praying for me and that I needed to start praying for myself. You told me to ask God for what I wanted and then when we were both fed up and I no longer wanted to hear your answers, because they didn't reflect what I wanted to do, nor did they make sense to me at the time, you told me to wait on God and do what God said...

I was ok with that at the time... because I really wasn't talking to God to even get an answer, I just didn't want to hear yours.

Then one day, I had to listen and those words you said, came forth in my spirit and they began to direct my life, persuade my decisions and position my prosperity.. that's the day I began to submit and allow Gods Word to advantage my life. I was now learning how to put my trust in God.

Life is so full of lesson and memorable moments... and as I memorialize all the moments, celebrations, disappointments and life changes that life served me... The one memory I will always treasure, is the Memory when you told me God Loved Me...

Thank You Mom for always being by my side... I will love you forever.

To Sheranda Myers (my cousin)

Sandy, Sugar Kane, Shay Shay all of these names people have given to you, I however know you as someone that was by my side when I needed a friend, someone by my side when every evil force raised its ugly head to kill, destroy, mislead and deceive me. You Sheranda have shared in supernatural encounters that would cause any man to go to a cliff and actually jump. The battles that we have won spiritually, the encounters we had to endure only could have been survived by someone that exhibited likeness in strength.

I know you as a listening ear, a giant in strength and a warrior in Christ. You have listened to every word I wrote, every book I edited, every disappointment I shared. You have watched tears fall from my face as I endured and almost lost my mind in spiritual warfare and you never complained or tired of me.

We have mirrored each other in so many situations and we even walked through time together, an experience no one would believe. Life has literally through difficult times served us a plate for Queens. The likeness in our strength can never be duplicated, our friendship to each other never replaced… you Sheranda, Sandy, Sugar Kane and Shay, Shay will always be the cousin that preserved, endured, experienced and conquered what some might consider spiritual hell with me. We proved ourselves in the army of God together and when the spirit of the enemy raised its ugly head, as we triumph together in exhaustion, we also lifted our heads up in victory. There will never be another you, another me. You are not just my cousin or any of the names above, you are me, I am you, we are one in Christ, approved, confirmed, validated, authorized, legitimate, certified, confirmed, verified, authenticated and backed in the army of the Lord and we WIN...

I will forever be grateful, appreciative, acknowledgeable and thankful for you.

Thanks for always Listening...

Love Pamela

To Shawn Richard Johnson

I recognize your validity in conclusion of the relevancy of your participation in my development as I persevered through my trials. I recognize the accurate development skills you used to cultivate my growth. I respect and admire the elicit approach you practiced during our many encounters and the sense of protection I felt during my storms.

Shawn, your ability and the quality of your approach in over standing the obvious of a matured love rendered an achievement in the continued progression of my spiritual expansion and often solitary movement.

I recognize you today and acknowledge you after having reached what I believe to be a final condition in my psyche and I pause and understand the full benefit of what it means to help others unconsciously.

The anima that was prevalent in the subconsciousness of your own mind channeled from above, I believe influenced the positive push that was kept unknown.

Inspiration comes from God and the steps of a righteous man are ordered by Him.

In conclusion, not only am I acknowledging the Charitable Contribution you made as a servant of God to navigate my being perhaps unbeknown to you, because of Promise, Decree and Will, I am also acknowledging the perfected knowledge of the Love of God That Ordered It.

Thank you from my create and the Heavens above... I remain.

Pamela Denise Brown

Goodwill Ambassador

For

The Positive Cultivation Of

Children

Author

Publisher

Illustrator

Editor

Entrepreneur

Producer

www.ingramcontent.com/pod-product-compliance
Lightning Source LLC
Chambersburg PA
CBHW061732020426
42331CB00006B/1213